YOU Choose

Wait Your Turn, Tilly

Be Patient

Lisa Regan

It might be useful for parents or teachers to read our 'How to use this book' guide on pages 28–29 before looking at Tilly's dilemmas. The points for discussion on these pages are helpful to share with your child once you have read the book together.

First published in 2013 by Wayland

Wayland
338 Euston Road
London NW1 3BH

Wayland Australia
Level 17/207 Kent Street
Sydney, NSW 2000

Produced for Wayland by Calcium
Design: Emma DeBanks
Editor for Wayland: Victoria Brooker
Illustrations by Lucy Neale

British Library Cataloguing in Publication Data

Wait your turn, Tilley. — (You choose)
   1. Patience—Juvenile literature. 2. Interpersonal relations—Juvenile literature.
   I. Series
   302.3'4–dc23

ISBN: 978 0 7502 7708 2

Printed in China

Wayland is a division of Hachette Children's Books, an Hachette UK company.
www.hachette.co.uk

Contents

Hello, Tilly!

Tilly finds it hard to be **patient**.
She doesn't like waiting, or
letting others have their turn.
She gets so **excited** and wants
to do everything **right now**!

Follow Tilly as she finds herself in tricky situations in which she must choose to be patient.

Don't snatch, Tilly

Tilly's brother is playing a game.

Tilly wants to play but there is only one game.

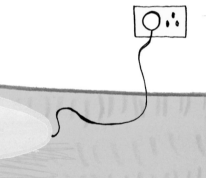

What should Tilly choose to do?

Should Tilly:

a **grab** the game and start to play?

b jump on her brother so that he can't play any more?

c ask if she can have a turn in five minutes?

Tilly, choose **c**

It's hard **sharing** toys and games. But grabbing will just **spoil** the fun for everyone. If you learn to share, everyone will be able to have a turn.

What would YOU choose to do?

Watch and wait, Tilly

Ryan and Jessica are playing on the seesaw in the park.

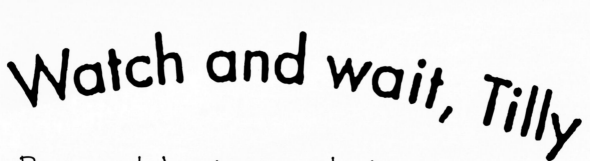

Tilly **loves** seesaws,
so she wants a go, too.

What should
Tilly choose
to do?

Should Tilly:

a play on the swings until one of the seesaw seats is free?

b scream and cry until she gets a go?

c push one of the children off the seat?

Tilly, choose **a**

Imagine how you would feel if you never got a turn. That's just how it feels to others if you keep things for yourself all of the time. Try to find something else that's fun to do while you wait your turn.

What would **you** choose to do?

13

Just wait, Tilly

Emily's birthday party has finished and her Mum is giving out the party bags.

Tilly **can't wait** to see all the goodies inside!

What should Tilly choose to do?

Should Tilly:

a push to the front of the **queue** so that she gets a bag first?

b wait with her friends because everyone will get a bag eventually?

c snatch a bag from another child?

Tilly, choose **b**

Try not to get so excited that you forget to be **polite**. If everyone is going to get a gift, it really doesn't matter who gets one first. Wait your turn – then people will see how patient you can be.

What would **YOU** choose to do?

That's selfish, Tilly

Tilly and Lucy are listening to music together on the CD player.

Lucy is really enjoying the song, but Tilly just **hates** it!

What should Tilly choose to do?

Should Tilly:

a turn off the music and say that they are going to do something else?

b push her friend away so she can choose a song?

C ask her friend to help her choose the next song?

Tilly, choose **C**

Be kind and try not to spoil your friend's fun. You can have your turn next. Playing with friends is always more fun if you take turns to choose what to do. Try to be patient – and wait your turn.

What would YOU choose to do?

Don't interrupt, Tilly

Tilly's Mum and Dad are
talking about grown-up things.

Tilly wants to tell them about **her** swimming lesson.

What should Tilly choose to do?

Should Tilly:

a **interrupt** and talk over the grown-ups?

b wait until they stop talking, and then say she has something to tell them?

c shout until they stop
their **conversation**
to listen to her?

Tilly, choose **b**

Grown-ups want to hear your
news, but they have things
they need to tell each other,
too. If they know you want to
talk, they will stop to listen to
your story. If you interrupt,
they will just feel cross.

What would
YOU
choose
to do?

Well done, Tilly!

Hey, look at Tilly! Now she can think of other people first, she's feeling much **happier**.

Did you choose the right thing to do? If you did, big cheers for you!

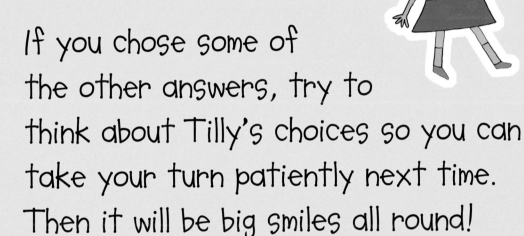

If you chose some of the other answers, try to think about Tilly's choices so you can take your turn patiently next time. Then it will be big smiles all round!

And remember – don't be impatient, wait your turn!

How to use this book

This book can be used by a grown-up and a child together. It is based on common situations that pose a challenge to all children. Invite your child to talk about each of the choices. Ask questions such as 'Why do you think Tilly should wait in line to get a party bag?'.

Discuss the wrong choices, as well as the right ones, with your child. Describe what is happening in the following pictures and talk about what the wrong and right choices might be.

● Don't hurt others. You shouldn't push or hit people to get what you want.

● Don't expect to get your own way the whole time. Other people are as important as you.

● Learn to take turns. That's the fairest way to share things such as toys.

● Listen to other people, and wait for for them to stop talking before you speak. It makes it hard to hear if two people talk at the same time.

Talk about and act out the situations in which a child might be impatient. Discuss what can be gained by waiting – it isn't always clear to young children, and they may have lots of questions that are difficult to answer. Try to show them that it's easy to push in, but people will like them a lot more if they choose to wait.

Discuss how upsetting or annoying it can be when someone always wants their own way. Ask them if they know anyone like that, and how it makes them feel. Ask them to think of better ways to behave that allow others to feel happy, too. Explain to your child that by learning to consider others, they will make more friends, which will make them happier, too.

Glossary

conversation when two or more people talk to each other

excited to feel thrilled about something

grab to take something in a rude way, without asking for it

imagine to think about what something might be like

interrupt to talk when someone else is talking

patient to wait without getting cross

polite to have good manners

queue to line up while waiting for something

sharing taking turns with other people so that everyone has a go

spoil to damage something

Index

Titles in the series

ISBN: 978 0 7502 7706 8

Like all children, Annie sometimes gets really, really angry! She has lots of choices to make – but which are the CALM ones?

ISBN: 978 0 7502 6724 3

Like all children, Carlos sometimes does things that are wrong, and doesn't come clean. He has lots of choices to make – but which are the TRUTHFUL ones?

ISBN: 978 0 7502 6722 9

Like all children, Charlie sometimes feels a little scared. He has lots of choices to make – but which are the BRAVE ones?

ISBN: 978 0 7502 6725 0

Like all children, Gertie sometimes plays a little dirty. We put Gertie on the spot with some tricky problems and ask her to decide what is FAIR!

ISBN: 978 0 7502 6723 6

Like all children, Harry sometimes takes things that don't belong to him. He has lots of choices to make – but which are the HONEST ones?

ISBN: 978 0 7502 7709 9

Like all children, Henry sometimes gets angry and sometimes he hits, too. He has lots of choices to make – but which are the GENTLE ones?

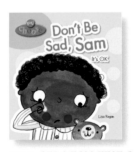

ISBN: 978 0 7502 7707 5

Like all children, Sam sometimes feels sad, and he doesn't know how to make himself feel better. He has lots of choices to make – but which are the HAPPY ones?

ISBN: 978 0 7502 7708 2

Like all children, Tilly wants to do everything *right now*, and sometimes she just can't wait! She has lots of choices to make – but which are the PATIENT ones?